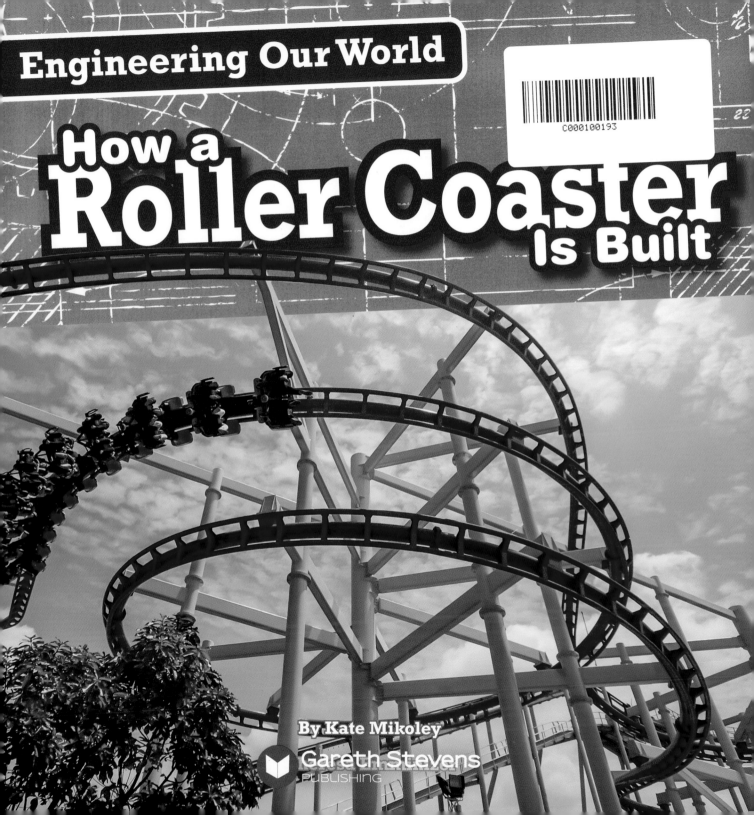

# Engineering Our World

# How a Roller Coaster Is Built

By Kate Mikoley

**Gareth Stevens**
PUBLISHING

Please visit our website, www.garethstevens.com. For a free color catalog of all our high-quality books, call toll free 1-800-542-2595 or fax 1-877-542-2596.

**Library of Congress Cataloging-in-Publication Data**

Names: Mikoley, Kate, author.
Title: How a roller coaster is built / Kate Mikoley.
Description: New York : Gareth Stevens Publishing, 2021. | Series: Engineering our world | Includes index. | Contents: A Wild Ride – Building Ice Slides – Plan It Out – All Kinds of Energy – Wooden Wonders – Super Steel – Lots of Loops – Riding the Ride – Build Your Own Loop.
Identifiers: LCCN 2019028471 | ISBN 9781538247075 (paperback) | ISBN 9781538247082 | ISBN 9781538247099 (library binding) | ISBN 9781538247105 (ebook)
Subjects: LCSH: Roller coasters–Design and construction–Juvenile literature.
Classification: LCC GV1860.R64 M55 2020 | DDC 791.06/8028–dc23
LC record available at https://lccn.loc.gov/2019028471

First Edition

Published in 2021 by
**Gareth Stevens Publishing**
111 East 14th Street, Suite 349
New York, NY 10003

Designer: Sarah Liddell
Editor: Monika Davies

Photo credits: Cover, p. 1 SIHASAKPRACHUM/Shutterstock.com; background Jason Winter/ Shutterstock.com; p. 5 Paper Cat/Shutterstock.com; p. 7 DE AGOSTINI PICTURE LIBRARY/ Contributor/De Agostini/Getty Images; p. 9 (main) Christian Bertrand/Shutterstock.com; p. 9 (inset) Ruslan Kerimov/Shutterstock.com; p. 11 VIAVAL/Shutterstock.com; p. 13 Marcio Jose Bastos Silva/Shutterstock.com; p. 15 Benson HE/Shutterstock.com; p. 17 Neale Cousland/ Shutterstock.com; p. 19 Andrey Mihaylov/Shutterstock.com; p. 20 (masking tape) Mega Pixel/ Shutterstock.com; p. 20 (scissors) macondo/Shutterstock.com; p. 20 (marble) SUFRI SARUDIN/ Shutterstock.com; pp 20, 21 (pool noodle) Pashin Georgiy/Shutterstock.com.

Printed in the United States of America
Some of the images in this book illustrate individuals who are models. The depictions do not imply actual situations or events.

CPSIA compliance information: Batch #CS20GS: For further information contact Gareth Stevens, New York, New York at 1-800-542-2595.

# Contents

A Wild Ride . . . . . . . . . . . . . . . . . . . . . . . . . . . . . . . . . . 4

Building Ice Slides . . . . . . . . . . . . . . . . . . . . . . . . . . . . 6

Plan It Out . . . . . . . . . . . . . . . . . . . . . . . . . . . . . . . . . . . 8

All Kinds of Energy . . . . . . . . . . . . . . . . . . . . . . . . . . . 10

Wooden Wonders . . . . . . . . . . . . . . . . . . . . . . . . . . . . 12

Super Steel . . . . . . . . . . . . . . . . . . . . . . . . . . . . . . . . . 14

Lots of Loops . . . . . . . . . . . . . . . . . . . . . . . . . . . . . . . 16

Riding the Ride . . . . . . . . . . . . . . . . . . . . . . . . . . . . . . 18

Build Your Own Loop . . . . . . . . . . . . . . . . . . . . . . . . . 20

Glossary . . . . . . . . . . . . . . . . . . . . . . . . . . . . . . . . . . . 22

For More Information . . . . . . . . . . . . . . . . . . . . . . . . . 23

Index . . . . . . . . . . . . . . . . . . . . . . . . . . . . . . . . . . . . . . 24

Words in the glossary appear in **bold** type the first time they are used in the text.

# A Wild Ride

When you're walking through the amusement park and the screams start to get louder, you can bet you're getting close to a roller coaster. Roller coasters come in all shapes and sizes—from old wooden rides with sharp turns to fancy steel coasters with huge drops and big **loops**!

No matter what kind of roller coaster you like to ride, a lot of planning and hard work went into building it. A science called **physics** plays an important part in engineering these thrilling rides.

## Building Blocks

Engineering is the use of science and math to plan and build better objects.

AMUSEMENT PARKS ARE PLACES WITH LOTS OF GAMES AND RIDES. THERE ARE USUALLY ONE OR MORE ROLLER COASTERS AT THESE PARKS!

# Building Ice Slides

Before roller coasters, there were rides called ice slides in Russia. People used wood to build hills that were then covered in ice. Those brave enough to go for a ride rode on wooden sleds or blocks of ice down these hills. They could reach speeds of about 50 miles (80 km) per hour!

Some people say ice slides sparked the idea for roller coasters. Later, **devices** such as wheels, tracks, and chains were added to make the coasters we know today.

## Building Blocks

In 1804, ice sliding came to Paris, France, as a ride named the Russian Mountains. This ride featured sleds with small wheels added on. Some people consider this the first wheeled roller coaster.

THIS ENGRAVING, OR DRAWING CUT INTO A HARD SURFACE, SHOWS A RUSSIAN ICE SLIDE IN ACTION. THE ICE SLIDES WERE NICKNAMED "FLYING MOUNTAINS."

# Plan It Out

Today's roller coasters feature big drops, quick turns, and changing speeds. On these coasters, trains of cars filled with people roll down rails. Without the drops, twists, and turns, your favorite coaster would just be a train ride!

One of the first steps to building a coaster is to create a design, or plan for how it will be made. Engineers use math and science to figure out everything in a coaster's design—from how high the big drop should be to how many people can ride at once.

## Building Blocks

Roller coasters need to be more than just fun—they also need to be safe. Engineers must work out how to build a structure that **supports** the coaster train's weight and speed.

MODERN ROLLER COASTERS HAVE WHEELS THAT GO ON THE TOP, BOTTOM, AND SIDE OF THE TRACK TO MAKE SURE THE TRAIN OF CARS NEVER LEAVES THE TRACK—EVEN ON THE SHARPEST TURNS!

9

# All Kinds of Energy

If you've ever seen a roller coaster, you've probably noticed that the biggest hill is set up at the beginning of the ride. Have you ever wondered why?

Roller coasters don't have engines. Instead, they get their **energy** for motion from that first climb up the hill. A special chain lift often pulls the train of cars up the first hill. This builds the train's potential energy, or energy that hasn't yet been used. When the train goes down the first hill, the build-up of energy is **released** as kinetic energy.

## Building Blocks

Kinetic energy is a kind of energy that comes from being in motion. This release of energy is how roller coaster trains can go up more hills after the first drop.

GRAVITY, OR THE FORCE THAT PULLS OBJECTS TOWARD EARTH'S CENTER, IS WHAT PULLS THE TRAIN OF CARS DOWN THE FIRST HILL.

# Wooden Wonders

There are now many different kinds of roller coasters, but they can be sorted into two main groups: wooden coasters and steel coasters.

The first roller coasters were made of wood. Wooden roller coasters need big support systems. These systems are commonly made of pieces of wood placed at different angles. Steel is also used for some parts of wooden coasters, such as the rails and parts of the support system. However, the track for these coasters is made of wood.

## Building Blocks

The strong bases of wooden roller coaster supports are usually made from concrete, or a mix of water, stones, sand, and a soft gray powder that becomes very hard and strong when it dries.

OVER TIME, WOOD CAN ROT. THE WOOD THAT MAKES UP THESE ROLLER COASTERS IS OFTEN TREATED WITH SPECIAL CHEMICALS TO PREVENT ROTTING.

# Super Steel

Today, some of the most hair-raising coasters are made of steel. Steel makes for a much smoother ride than wood. Plus, steel coasters often have sharper twists and turns.

Wood can be cut to make turns in a ride, but it's only able to bend a certain amount. However, steel can be heated and bent into the best shape for the ride's design. Steel parts for a coaster are often made somewhere else. They're then taken to the amusement park where workers put the coaster together piece by piece.

## Building Blocks

Steel can handle more weight and force than wood can. That's why steel coasters can have much higher and steeper drops!

STEEL ROLLER COASTERS OFTEN HAVE TUBULAR, OR ROUNDED, TRACKS. THESE TRACKS WERE INVENTED IN THE 1950S AND ALSO OFTEN HAVE TUBULAR SUPPORTS AS WELL.

# Lots of Loops

You might think seat belts are why people stay in their seats when coasters go upside down. But that's only part of the reason! As the train goes around the loop, **inertia** is a force that pushes you toward the outside of the loop, working against gravity to keep you in your seat.

When you're upside down on a loop, you may feel almost weightless. That's because gravity is pulling you toward the ground while inertia is pulling you toward the top of the loop.

## Building Blocks

Engineers make coaster loops into oval shapes. If loops were perfect circles, the forces pushing against you wouldn't feel comfortable and the ride also wouldn't be safe.

THE LOOPS IN A MODERN ROLLER COASTER ARE OFTEN SHAPED LIKE AN OVAL WITH A POINT AT THE BOTTOM. THIS SHAPE IS CALLED A TEARDROP DESIGN.

17

# Riding the Ride

An engineer's work isn't done once the roller coaster has been built. They must then test the roller coaster to make sure they've done their job correctly and made a safe ride.

The first riders of a new roller coaster often aren't people. They're usually bags of sand or dummies. If these objects stay in place and make it through the ride safely, the coaster can then be tested with people. The next riders can be those who designed the ride or other workers at the park.

## Building Blocks

From designing the ride to putting it in place, building a roller coaster can sometimes take up to 5 years!

ENGINEERS ARE ALWAYS USING THE LATEST SCIENCE TO MAKE MORE DELIGHTFUL RIDES. SOME ROLLER COASTERS CAN NOW REACH SPEEDS OVER 100 MILES (161 KM) PER HOUR!

# Build Your Own Loop

Now that you know what goes into making a roller coaster, you can make your own loop!

## What You Need:

- foam tube (such as a pool noodle)

- masking tape

- marble, or a small glass ball

- scissors

## How To Do It:

1. Use scissors to cut the foam tube in half lengthwise to create a track and tape it open. Ask an adult for help.

2. Make a loop for your roller coaster using one half of the tube. Leave room for the track to **extend** before and after the loop. Tape one end of the tube in place.

3. Tape the beginning of the track to a table or chair that's higher to make the coaster's drop.

4. Let the marble roll down the drop on the track.

5. If your marble doesn't fully make it around your coaster's loop, try changing the height of the drop or the size of the loop.

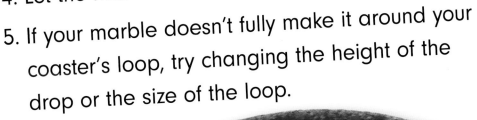

# Glossary

**chemical:** matter that can be mixed with other matter to cause changes

**device:** a tool or machine made to accomplish a task

**energy:** power used to do work

**extend:** to stretch out

**inertia:** a property of matter by which something that is moving in a direction continues moving in that direction at the same speed until another force acts on it

**loop:** a curved shape created when something bends around in a way so it crosses over itself

**physics:** the study of matter, energy, force, and motion, and the relationship among them

**release:** to set something free

**support:** to hold up something

# For More Information

## Books

Kenney, Karen Latchana. *The Science of Roller Coasters: Understanding Energy*. Minneapolis, MN: Abdo Publishing, 2016.

LeBoutillier, Linda. *Unusual and Awesome Jobs Using Technology: Roller Coaster Designer, Space Robotics Engineer, and More*. North Mankato, MN: Capstone Press, 2015.

Pettiford, Rebecca. *Roller Coasters*. Minneapolis, MN: Jump!, 2016

## Websites

### Design a Roller Coaster
*www.learner.org/interactives/parkphysics/coaster*
Use what you've learned to design your own coaster. When you're done, find out if your choices make for a safe and fun ride!

### How Do Roller Coasters Work?
*www.wonderopolis.org/wonder/how-do-roller-coasters-work*
Find out more about how roller coasters work on this website.

### Why Don't I Fall Out When a Roller Coaster Goes Upside Down?
*www.loc.gov/rr/scitech/mysteries/rollercoaster.html*
Learn more about the physics of roller coaster loops here.

# Index

amusement park  4, 5, 14

cars  8, 9, 10, 11

chain  6, 10

concrete  12

design  8, 14, 17, 18

engineers  8, 16, 18, 19

force  11, 14, 16

gravity  11, 16

hill  6, 10, 11

ice slides  6, 7

kinetic energy  10

loop  4, 16, 17, 20, 21

Paris, France  6

physics  4

potential energy  10

rails  8, 12

rotting  13

Russia  6

Russian Mountains  6

shape  4, 14, 16, 17

speed  6, 8, 19

steel roller coasters 4, 12, 14, 15

support  4, 12, 15

test  18

track  6, 9, 12, 15, 21

train  8, 9, 10, 11, 16

turns  4, 8, 9, 14

twists  8, 14

weight  8, 14, 16

wheels  6, 9

wooden roller coasters 4, 12